For Bethany, Sam, and Emily
—K.R.Y.

To my supportive wife, Lisa,
and my precious daughter, Meghan
—B.S.

Book copyright © 1996 Trudy Corporation, 353 Main Avenue, Norwalk, CT 06851, and the Smithsonian Institution, Washington, DC 20560.

Soundprints is a division of Trudy Corporation, Norwalk, Connecticut.

Book Design: Shields & Partners, Westport, CT

First Edition
10 9 8 7 6 5 4 3 2 1
Printed in Singapore

Acknowledgements:
    Our very special thanks to Dr. Charles Handley of the Department of Vertebrate Zoology at the Smithsonian's National Museum of Natural History for his curatorial review.

Library of Congress Cataloging-in-Publication Data

Young, Karen Romano.
    The ice's edge: the story of a harp seal pup / written by Karen Romano Young; illustrated by Brian Shaw.
        p.   cm.
    Summary: Shows what the life of a harp seal is like as he grows up.
        ISBN 1-56899-307-2
    1. Harp seal — Infancy — Juvenile literature. [1. Harp seal. 2. Seals (Animals)]
    I. Shaw, Brian, 1968- II. Title.
        QL737.P64Y68   1996   96-7323
        599.748—dc20   CIP
                                                                              AC

THE ICE'S EDGE

The Story of a Harp Seal Pup

by Karen Romano Young   Illustrated by Brian Shaw

Soundprints

Where Children Discover...

Off the coast of Labrador, a hungry harp seal pup lies on the ice gazing at the cloudy March sky. His fluffy fur glimmers as white as the snow around him. His enormous eyes glow as black as the dark ocean water below.

Little Harp Seal rolls onto his stomach, peers into a hole in the ice, and cries. His mother is down there somewhere! "Ow-ooo!"

Mother pops out of her breathing hole and sniffs Little Harp Seal's muzzle. There are hundreds of other baby seals on the ice, but from this "kiss" she knows he is hers.

Little Harp Seal smells his mother's milk, and he nudges her flank until he finds it. Just three days old, he is already an expert at nursing.

Here, on the pack ice, the females give birth to their pups every winter. Mother chose this spot when the ice was thin. She kept a hole open as the ice grew thicker to use as her doorway to the sea.

Full of milk, Little Harp Seal lolls like a sleepy white blimp. He is almost asleep when the growling of the older seals startles him. A hungry polar bear is stalking on silent, fur-padded feet.

Mother and many of the other adults slip quietly into the water. The babies' white fur blends in with the ice, but the polar bear can spot the mothers' gray coats from far away.

Alone, Little Harp Seal stays motionless as the bear moves closer.

Plonk! An adult seal dives through a breathing hole behind the polar bear. The bear turns toward the sound, then looks back at Little Harp Seal. To him, Little Harp Seal looks like just another lump of ice. At last, the bear decides there is nothing to eat here and lumbers away.

As the days pass, Little Harp Seal eats, sleeps, and grows. A thick layer of blubber forms under his skin to protect him from the cold. His puppy fur helps by trapping warm sunshine. But spring is coming. Soon the pack ice will melt and the seals will be without a home.

One morning as Little Harp Seal sleeps, Mother wakes early and slithers into her breathing hole. It is not long before other mothers slide into the water. Together, the mothers swim away to find mates and make their long journey to the ice pack near Greenland.

Little Harp Seal wakes alone, hungry. All morning he calls for his mother, growing hungrier by the minute. The air is filled with pitiful cries as other pups search for their mothers. No one answers them.

A few days later, Little Harp Seal's fur begins to change. His soft white coat falls out in clumps. Beneath it, sleek silvery fur appears, dotted with dark gray.

Another pup slides up beside him. She follows Little Harp Seal as he squirms over to his mother's old breathing hole. Together, they look over the edge, yelping, leaning toward the water, searching —

Splash!

The seal pups tumble into the hole.
The icy water closes over Little Harp Seal's
head. He opens his mouth to cry out and
gets a mouthful of sea water. Coughing and
gasping with surprise, Little Harp Seal bobs
to the surface and breathes deeply.

20

The pups paddle the water frantically, trying to climb out of the breathing hole. Little Harp Seal's blubber helps him float. His strong, webbed hind flippers beat the water.

He can swim!

He dives down, his sleek new fur helping him slide through the water easily. Nearby, the other pup begins to swim, too.

Little Harp Seal's large eyes take in all the light that passes through the water, allowing him to see into the darkest corners. Mother Seal is nowhere to be found.

A fluttering vibration reaches Little Harp Seal's whiskers as he weaves along just below the surface. He grabs with his mouth and comes up with krill — tiny creatures that drift through the water. Little Harp Seal has caught his first meal.

The seal pups spend their days together, practicing their swimming and fishing, and dozing on the ice. One day while Little Harp Seal is fishing, the other pup strikes out for the north, seeking colder waters and a new home on solid ice.

Little Harp Seal emerges from the breathing hole to find someone else waiting for him. Bluish-white fur, enormous teeth, and a horrible growl greet the little seal. The polar bear prepares to attack.

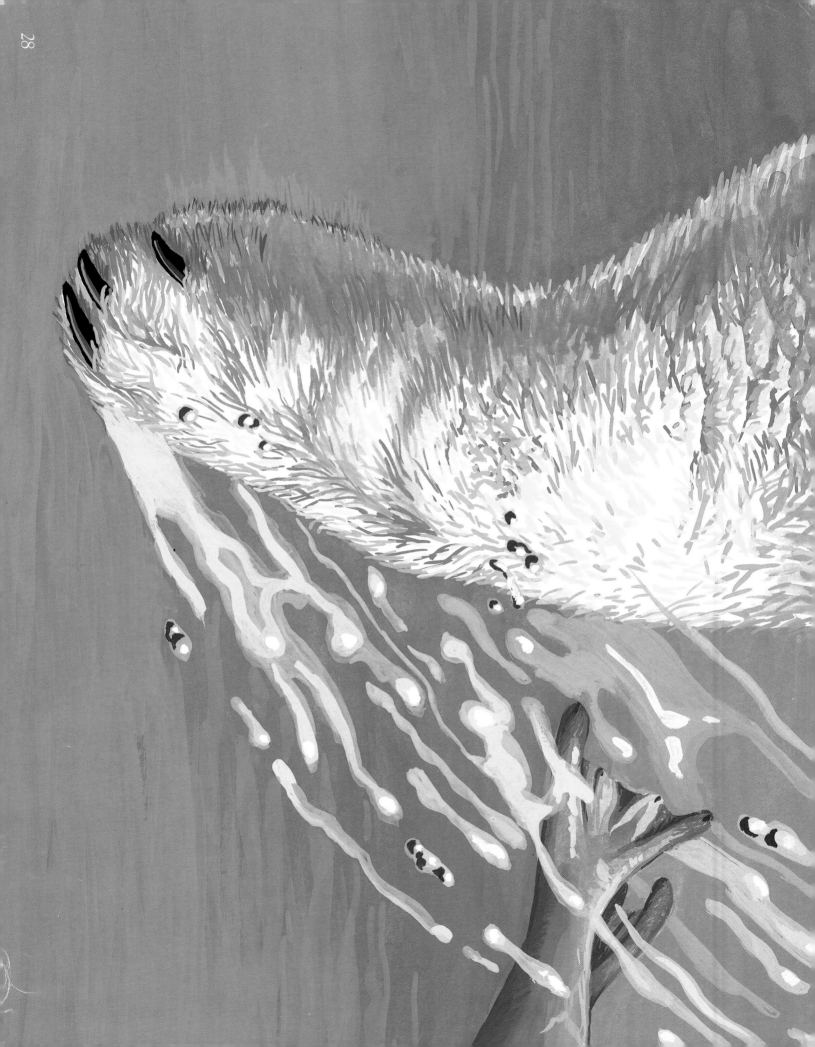

A giant white paw sweeps into the water, and Little Harp Seal plunges down in terror. He escapes the bear's sharp claws, but he can't hold his breath for long. Little Harp Seal darts up to the surface, desperate for air. He draws a deep breath, spies the bear's nose, and dives again.

Little Harp Seal swims beneath the ice, searching for a way out. He spots another breathing hole and surfaces far from the bear.

Slipping up onto the ice, Little Harp Seal lies by his new breathing hole. His sleek gray coat stands out against the cold white snow. He no longer needs his baby fur to hide him — he can take care of himself.

Soon, he too will journey to colder waters in the north. He will follow the route that Harp Seals have swum for thousands of years. He will follow the ice's edge.

About the Harp Seal

Harp seals, also known as *pagophilus*, or ice-loving, seals, live their entire lives on and near sea ice. Born inactive and helpless, harp seal pups first sport fluffy, yellowish fur. When they are two or three days old, the yellow coat fades and becomes transparent, absorbing the sun's light for warmth and at the same time, appearing white as it blends with the ice and snow. After three to four weeks, the pups are weaned and their transparent fur turns spotted gray. At this age, the pups are known as "beaters" for their awkward swimming style — beating the water's surface with their front flippers to stay afloat.

Later in the spring, the "beaters" migrate north to join other seals near the pack ice of the Arctic. Along the way, the seals are in danger of being eaten by sharks and orca whales. Adult harp seals, called "saddlebacks," are strong swimmers. They can hold their breath for 30 minutes and dive to depths up to 600 feet. Some harp seals will swim over 3,000 miles a year, following food trails of small fish.

For two hundred years, newborn harp seals were hunted for their fluffy white coats, until commercial hunting of "white coats" was banned in 1988 after a public outcry.

Glossary

breathing hole: a hole made by a seal in the ice for access between water and air.

flank: an area on the side of an animal, behind the ribs.

flipper: a wide, flat limb that is used for swimming.

krill: small crustaceans that float in the water — a source of food for many seals, whales, fish, and seabirds.

pack ice: sea ice broken into plates by ocean swells and formed into large masses, crushed and piled together by wind and waves.

vibration: a tiny movement of the water caused by motion.

Points of Interest in this Book